"... like a fabulous silvery fish, floating quietly in the ocean of air ..."
—*Hugo Eckener*

For Eamon, Evan, and Eileen
at the start of their voyage

——————

Henry Holt and Company, LLC
Publishers since 1866, 115 West 18th Street, New York, New York 10011

Henry Holt is a registered trademark of Henry Holt and Company, LLC
Copyright © 2000 by Patrick O'Brien. All rights reserved.
Distributed in Canada by H. B. Fenn and Company Ltd.

Library of Congress Cataloging-in-Publication Data
O'Brien, Patrick. The Hindenburg / Patrick O'Brien
Summary: Describes the development and early flights of airships and the disastrous crash of
the *Hindenburg* at an airfield in New Jersey in 1937. 1. *Hindenburg* (Airship)—Juvenile literature.
2. Airships—Juvenile literature. 3. Aircraft accidents—New Jersey—Juvenile literature.
[1. *Hindenburg* (Airship). 2. Airships. 3. Aircraft accidents.] 1. Title.
TL659.H5 O27 2000 629.133'25—dc21 99-46687
ISBN 0-8050-6415-X / First Edition—2000 / Designed by Donna Mark
Printed in the United States of America on acid-free paper. ∞
3 5 7 9 10 8 6 4 2

The artist used watercolor and gouache on Italian watercolor
paper to create the illustrations for this book.

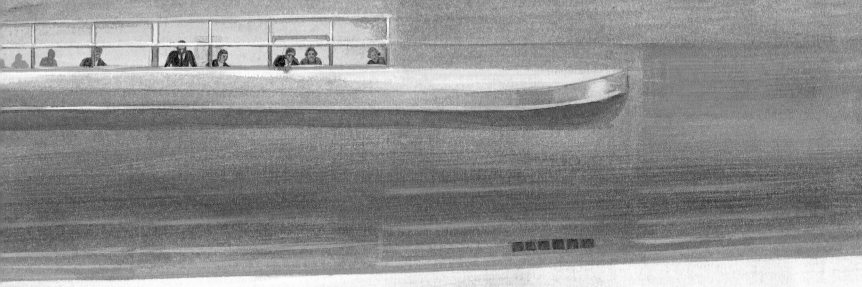

THE
Hindenburg

PATRICK O'BRIEN

HENRY HOLT AND COMPANY
NEW YORK

"Up ship!" shouted the captain, and the mighty airship floated free. The passengers gathered at the windows, watching the airfield fall away below them. This was the start of a grand voyage that would take them westward from Germany and over the wide Atlantic Ocean. In three days, the *Hindenburg* would be in America.

Hugo Eckener had made his dream come true. He had dedicated his life to airships. Now at last he had created the perfect airship—the most modern, the most luxurious, the fastest, the largest.

People loved the gigantic ship. Cities erupted in cheers when it flew overhead. Hundreds of thousands of people waited for hours just to see it. For the passengers who flew on the *Hindenburg,* the experience was unforgettable. "Yes," Eckener said, "an airship voyage is wonderful."

Hugo Eckener

But on May 6, 1937, at the end of the first flight of the new flying season, something went terribly wrong.

It was four in the morning, and Hugo Eckener was fast asleep. The telephone on the bedside table rang, and Eckener reached for it groggily. "I felt it necessary to inform you," said the man on the other end, "that the *Hindenburg* exploded yesterday evening . . . above the airfield at Lakehurst, New Jersey."

"That can't be!" said Eckener. But the next day, newspapers around the world told the tragic story of the destruction of the *Hindenburg*. Was this the end of his whole life's work?

Eckener's fascination with airships had begun back in 1900 when he was still a young man. He lived in southern Germany, where a rich eccentric adventurer by the name of Count Ferdinand von Zeppelin was inventing a new way to fly.

At that time, the airplane had not yet been invented. The only way to fly was with a balloon. But balloons could go only where the winds would take them. Count Zeppelin wanted to make a balloon that could be steered.

Count Zeppelin

Count Zeppelin came up with the curious idea of putting several balloons inside a hollow, rigid structure, and then adding engines for power and fins for steering. The word *dirigible* means "able to be steered." The "crazy old Count's" steerable airships soon became known as dirigibles.

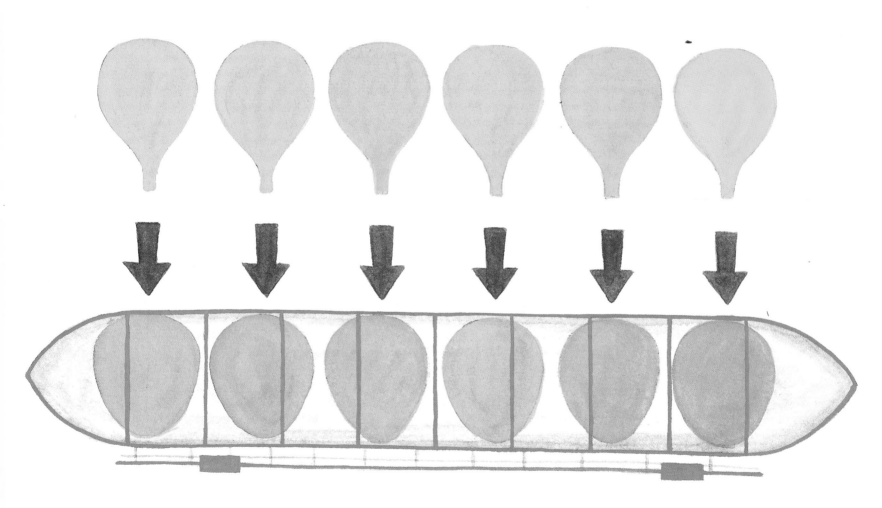

Count Zeppelin tested his first dirigible in July 1900. For eighteen minutes he flew his invention above Lake Constance in Germany before making an emergency landing on the water.

Hugo Eckener was not impressed. He thought that the flight was an interesting experiment and nothing more. But when he met the inventor, Eckener said, he "fell under the spell of Count Zeppelin and his ideas." He joined Zeppelin's company, and soon became their best airship pilot.

Count Zeppelin continued to build and test his dirigibles. There were many accidents in those early days, but the Count never gave up.

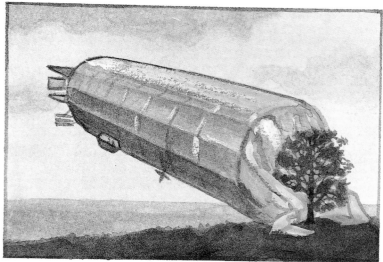

Zeppelin learned from his mistakes. He improved his dirigibles, and flying became safe and routine. Between 1911 and 1914, his dirigibles made 1,600 flights around Germany and carried more than 34,000 passengers.

The German people loved the big, strange airships that floated through the skies like huge silver whales. Count Zeppelin became a national hero, and his wondrous new dirigibles came to be called zeppelins.

Count Zeppelin, however, was a military man at heart. His vision for dirigibles was to carry bombs, not passengers. Soon enough, he would have a chance to show the world how his zeppelins could rain destruction on the enemy below.

World War I broke out in 1914. Germany was on one side and England was on the other. In the dark of night, fleets of German zeppelins would sail stealthily toward England. Over the city of London, the crewmen dropped bombs on the unsuspecting people below. This was a new and cruel type of warfare. Never before had a city been bombed from the air.

At the beginning of the war, the English had no defense against this new airborne menace. But they soon developed high-flying airplanes that carried machine guns with explosive bullets. The large, slow-moving zeppelins then became easy targets for the English fighter aces. During the war, more than half of the German zeppelins were destroyed by the enemy or in accidents.

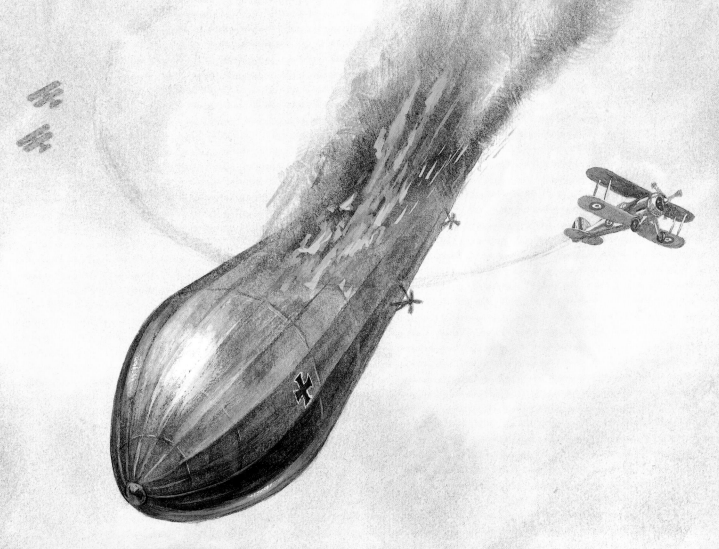

In 1918, Germany finally lost the war. Count Zeppelin did not live to see the failure of his invention as a military machine. He died in 1917 at the age of seventy-eight.

After the war, Eckener became the director of the Zeppelin Company. In 1928, the company built its biggest and most advanced dirigible so far, the *Graf Zeppelin*. With this ship, Eckener would show the world that his dream of safe, comfortable travel over the Atlantic Ocean on large passenger airships was possible. He flew the *Graf Zeppelin* on a round-trip voyage across the Atlantic to the United States. The dirigible carried twenty passengers in the height of luxury. Americans were wild with excitement, and gave Eckener a ticker-tape parade in Manhattan. Eckener happily declared that "a new world in technology had arrived!"

Tokyo, Japan

The Graf Zeppelin over Tokyo

In 1929, Eckener flew the *Graf Zeppelin* around the world. Everywhere it went the ship was greeted by huge crowds that flocked to see the amazing craft. The President of the United States, Herbert Hoover, proclaimed that Eckener was a "great adventurer like Columbus or Magellan."

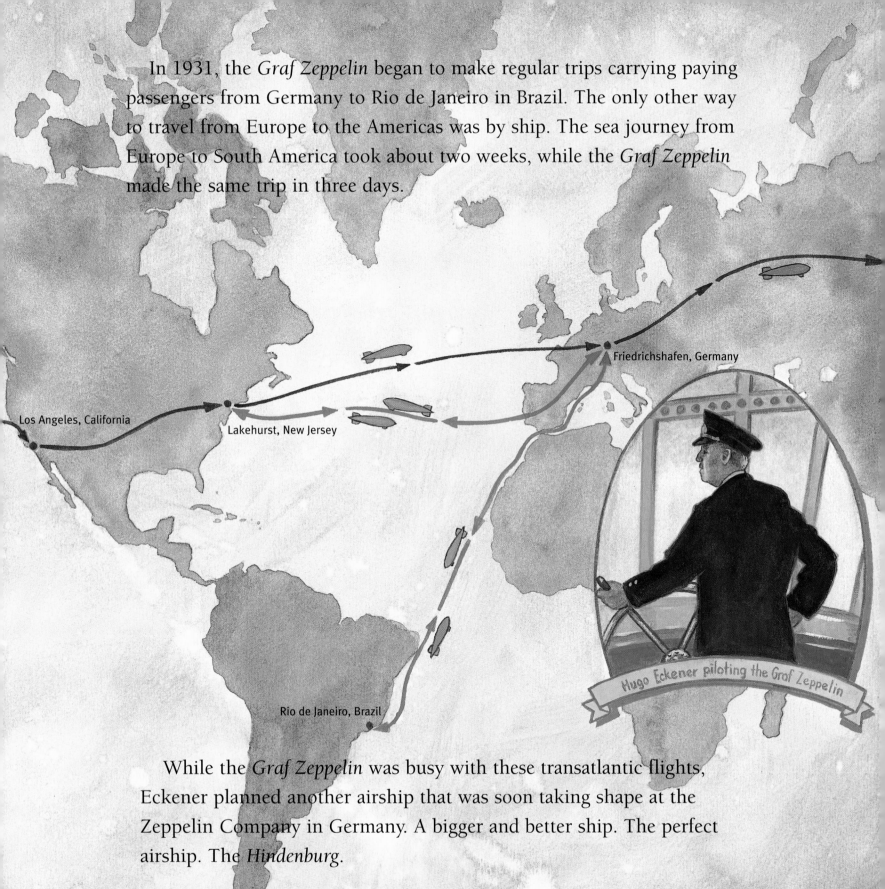

In 1931, the *Graf Zeppelin* began to make regular trips carrying paying passengers from Germany to Rio de Janeiro in Brazil. The only other way to travel from Europe to the Americas was by ship. The sea journey from Europe to South America took about two weeks, while the *Graf Zeppelin* made the same trip in three days.

Los Angeles, California

Lakehurst, New Jersey

Friedrichshafen, Germany

Rio de Janeiro, Brazil

Hugo Eckener piloting the Graf Zeppelin

While the *Graf Zeppelin* was busy with these transatlantic flights, Eckener planned another airship that was soon taking shape at the Zeppelin Company in Germany. A bigger and better ship. The perfect airship. The *Hindenburg*.

The new zeppelin was to be so big that a giant new hangar had to be made to house it.

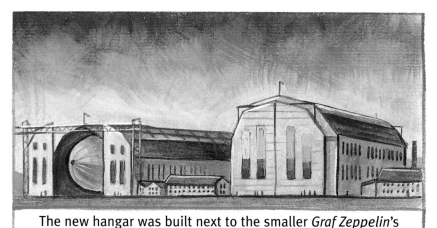

The new hangar was built next to the smaller *Graf Zeppelin*'s hangar, and then construction of the *Hindenburg* began.

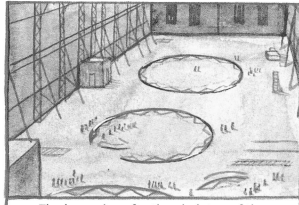

The large rings for the skeleton of the airship were constructed on the floor.

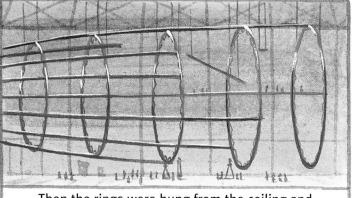

Then the rings were hung from the ceiling and connected with lengthwise girders.

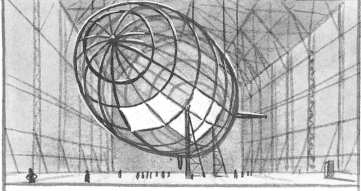

Once the "skeleton" was complete, a cotton fabric "skin" was stretched over it.

The skin was painted with "dope," a mixture of resins and aluminum flakes.

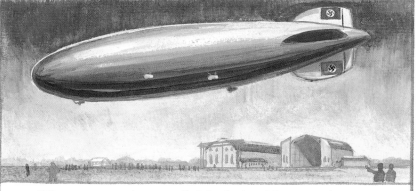

When construction was finished, the ship was taken on several test flights.

The gas cells in the *Hindenburg* were filled with hydrogen. Hydrogen can be extremely dangerous because it will explode if it comes into contact with a spark or a flame. All the German zeppelins ever made had been filled with hydrogen, but the zeppelin workers were very careful and they had an excellent safety record. In the early days there had been a few accidents in which crew members were killed, but no paying passenger had ever been hurt or killed in a German zeppelin accident.

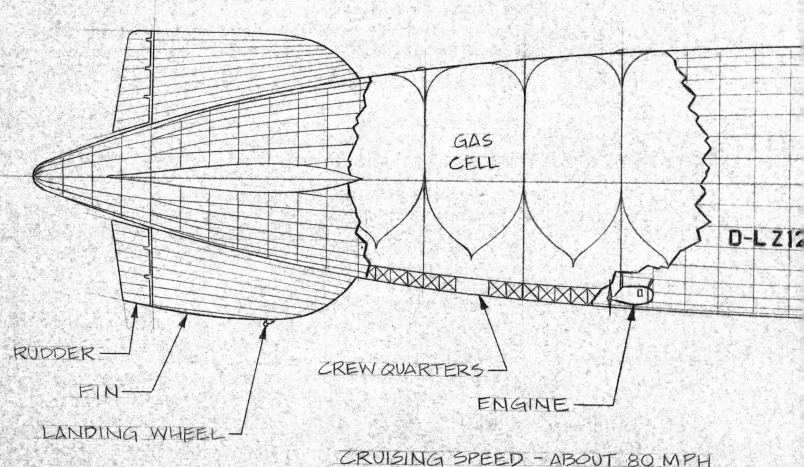

GAS CELL

D-LZ12

RUDDER

FIN

LANDING WHEEL

CREW QUARTERS

ENGINE

CRUISING SPEED — ABOUT 80 MPH
CRUISING HEIGHT — 650 TO 800 FEET

The designers of the *Hindenburg* included all the latest safety
measures in their new zeppelin. An American naval officer examined
the ship and reported, "I consider all possibilities of danger in the
new zeppelin eliminated."

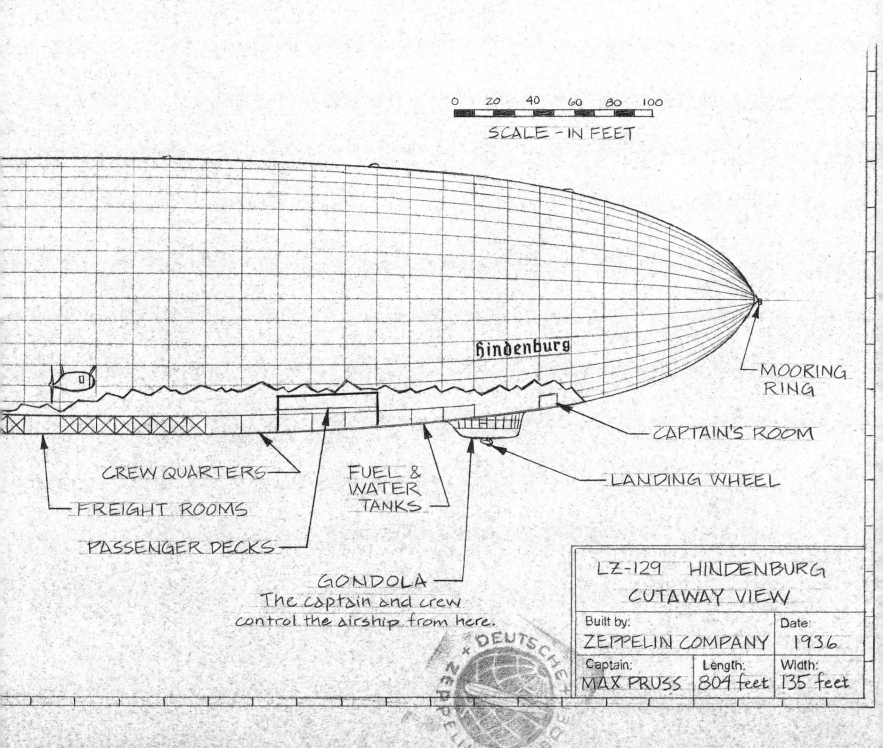

0 20 40 60 80 100
SCALE - IN FEET

hindenburg

MOORING RING

CAPTAIN'S ROOM

CREW QUARTERS

FREIGHT ROOMS

FUEL & WATER TANKS

LANDING WHEEL

PASSENGER DECKS

GONDOLA
The captain and crew
control the airship from here.

LZ-129 HINDENBURG CUTAWAY VIEW		
Built by: ZEPPELIN COMPANY		Date: 1936
Captain: MAX PRUSS	Length: 804 feet	Width: 135 feet

In the 1930s, the Nazis came into power in Germany. Eckener did not like their brutal ways. He resisted their control whenever he could, and he made speeches criticizing the Nazi party. Eckener thought that transatlantic travel could help create better understanding between different countries. He said that he wanted "to be of service to mankind in the development of air travel." But the Nazis wanted zeppelins only to glorify Germany and to symbolize Nazi power.

The Nazis did not like Eckener, so they made him a "nonperson." This meant that his name could not be mentioned in newspapers, and no one was allowed to print a picture of him. Eckener was forced to put the Nazi symbol, the swastika, on the *Hindenburg*. His dream airship would have to fly the Atlantic with the hated swastika displayed on the tail fins.

The *Hindenburg* made its first flight to America in May of 1936. The takeoff was so smooth that passengers did not even know the ship was airborne unless they were looking out the windows. The ride was perfectly steady and quiet as the ship cruised at 80 miles per hour over the Atlantic Ocean.

Only the rich could afford to travel by airship. The tickets were $400, about the price of a small car in those days. The passengers had their own rooms with beds and sinks, and there was even a shower on board. The kitchen was well stocked with the finest foods. On Atlantic crossings, the chefs used 440 pounds of meat and poultry, 800 eggs, and 220 pounds of butter.

When the airship arrived in America, cruising low over New York
City, thousands of people filled the rooftops, windowsills, and streets,
cheering wildly as the huge zeppelin floated overhead. Eckener later
tried to explain the strange appeal of his giant soaring ships. A zeppelin,
he said, was "like a fabulous silvery fish, floating quietly in the ocean of
air. . . . It seemed to be coming from another world and to be returning
there like a dream."

The *Hindenburg* made nine more round-trip flights to the United States in 1936. The landing spot was in Lakehurst, New Jersey, about an hour south of New York City. During the winter of that year, the *Hindenburg* made seven trips down to Rio de Janeiro.

The first flying season was a huge success, and eighteen trips to the United States were scheduled for the next year. At the same time, the Zeppelin Company's other ship, the *Graf Zeppelin*, was still keeping a schedule of regular flights from Germany to Rio de Janeiro.

Because of the success of the *Hindenburg*, Hugo Eckener was able to make an agreement with an American company. The Americans would build two big airships, and the Zeppelin Company in Germany would build two more. There would be four new airships flying the Atlantic. Eckener's dream of regular transatlantic travel was beginning to come true.

On May 3, 1937, sixty-one crew members and thirty-six passengers boarded the *Hindenburg* for the flight to America. Fourteen-year-old Werner Franz was thrilled to be a cabin boy on the famous airship. He was the youngest member of the crew. Two of the passengers were even younger—Werner and Wallace Doehner, ages six and eight. Somewhere over the Atlantic, a steward politely took away Werner's toy truck. It made sparks when it rolled. In an airship filled with explosive hydrogen, sparks could mean disaster.

The *Hindenburg* cruised low over the icebergs of the North Atlantic, close to the spot where the *Titanic* had gone down twenty-five years before. At four o'clock on the afternoon of May 6, the *Hindenburg* arrived over the landing field in Lakehurst, New Jersey. There were thunderstorms in the area, so it cruised south over the beaches of the Atlantic coast to wait out the storms.

Shortly after seven o'clock, the *Hindenburg* returned to the landing field and slowed to a stop about 250 feet above the ground. The crew dropped ropes from the ship's nose so the men below could help bring the ship in. Everything was done according to plan. It was a routine landing. There was no warning of what was about to happen.

In thirty-two seconds, the mighty airship *Hindenburg* was a mass of flaming wreckage on the ground.

Amazingly, of the ninety-seven people on board, sixty-seven survived the explosion. One person on the ground was killed, and five survivors died later in the hospital.

One passenger who was an acrobat was able to hang on outside a window of the burning airship until it was low enough that he could drop off onto the sandy ground below. He stood up, brushed himself off, and limped away. One older couple walked down the steps of the slowly falling ship as if it was a normal landing. They escaped, injured but alive. The Doehner brothers survived when their mother threw them out of a window into the arms of the rescuers below.

Werner Franz, the fourteen-year-old cabin boy, rode the flaming airship almost all the way to the ground. A large water tank in the ship above his head burst, drenching him with water. He jumped to the ground as the flaming airship was falling around him and dashed out, soaking wet but unharmed.

The cause of the *Hindenburg* explosion is still a mystery. Hugo Eckener felt that there was static electricity in the air because of the thunderstorms in the area, and that this electricity might have ignited some hydrogen that was leaking near the back of the airship. Some people believe, however, that a bomb caused the explosion. There was no evidence of a bomb, but the swastikas on the tail of the ship might have made the *Hindenburg* a target for people who wanted to destroy a symbol of Nazi power.

Millions of people around the world watched newsreels of the *Hindenburg* explosion and heard reports about it on the radio. Zeppelins were now seen as death traps, and all interest in building more of them died with the *Hindenburg*. Eckener wrote that "it appeared to me the hopeless end of a great dream, a kind of end of the world."

Over the years, airplanes have been developed to be much faster and bigger than they were before. People now fly in airplanes instead of airships. Even Hugo Eckener had to admit that "a good thing has been replaced by a better." The mighty zeppelins no longer cruise through the ocean of air on grand voyages to distant lands. Like the *Hindenburg*, the era of the great airships is gone forever.

DID YOU KNOW?

The *Hindenburg* made the trip from Germany to America in two and a half days. The only other way to cross the Atlantic was by ship, and the fastest ships needed five days to make the trip.

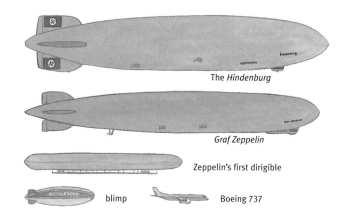

The *Hindenburg*

Graf Zeppelin

Zeppelin's first dirigible

blimp

Boeing 737

The *Hindenburg* was the biggest thing that ever flew.

On one return trip from Rio de Janeiro, someone sneaked five monkeys on board the *Graf Zeppelin*. They soon got loose and were seen swinging through the girders inside the airship.

Pets were shipped on the *Hindenburg*—dogs, birds, fish, and even a deer.

The *Hindenburg* was named for a former president of Germany, Paul von Hindenburg.

Airships docked at mooring masts. A ring on the front of an airship was attached to the top of the mast. This allowed the ship to swing with the wind while moored.

The tower on the top of the Empire State Building was built as a mooring mast. It was never used.

Play stopped at a baseball game between the Brooklyn Dodgers and the Pittsburgh Pirates in Brooklyn when the *Hindenburg* flew over on its way to a landing. Everyone wanted to watch the airship.

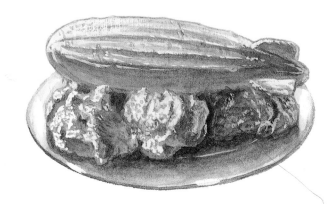

Eckener went to a party in New York City to celebrate the *Hindenburg*'s first flight. In the middle of the table was a mound of ice cream in the shape of a zeppelin.

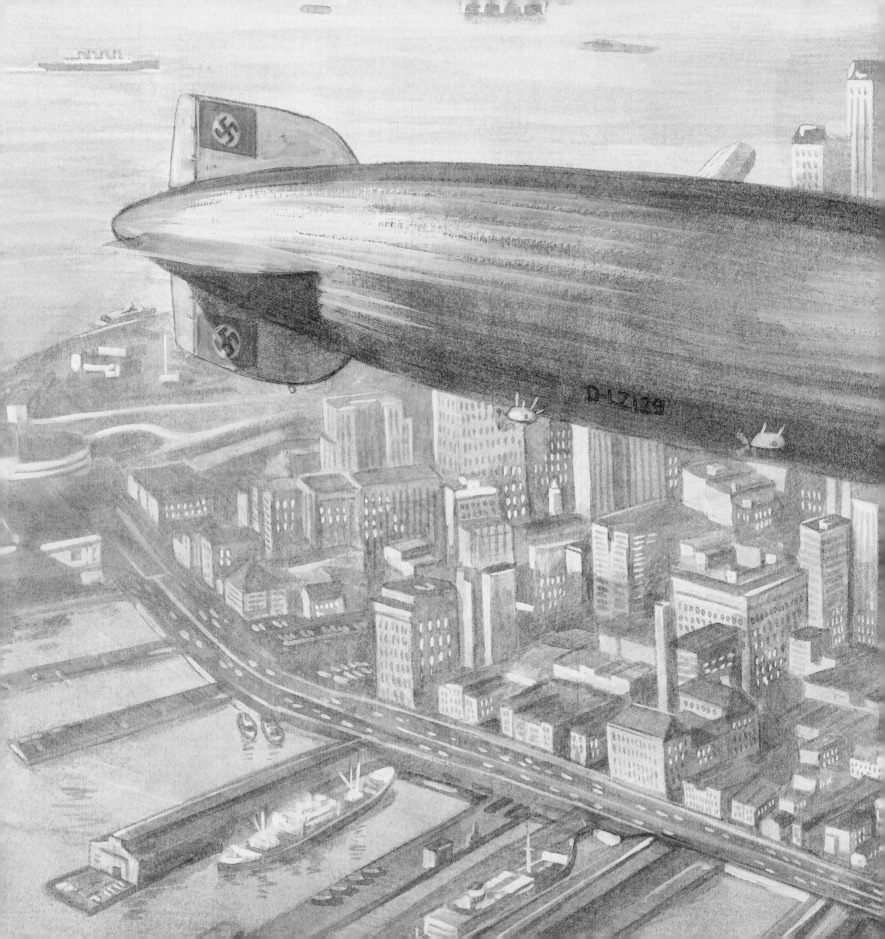